The Kids Hymnal

Presented To:

_____

From:

_____

The Kids Hymnal: 80 Songs and Hymns

Hendrickson Publishers, Inc.
P.O. Box 3473
Peabody, Massachusetts 01961-3473

ISBN 978-1-59856-214-9

Printed in China

Second printing—June 2009

Cover and interior illustrations by Tim O'Connor
Cover and interior design by Chad Stephens and Jay Elkins

The Kids Hymnal

HENDRICKSON
Worship

Table of Contents

Welcome to *The Kids Hymnal*

Kids love to sing. And they love singing hymns, especially with other kids!

The Kids Hymnal is a collection of 80 songs that your children will enjoy because they're familiar, fun, and full of faith. As parents, educators, and mentors, we can take that enjoyment one step further to build a solid foundation of Christian truths for children ages 4 to 10. Using **The Kids Hymnal**, we can present God's doctrines in a clear, understandable, age-appropriate, and entertaining way.

That's the whole idea behind **The Kids Hymnal**: to make God's Word and the messages of the Christian faith relevant to our kids. For each selection in **The Kids Hymnal**, children not only learn the song but also discover the song's meaning, adopt the spiritual affirmation that accompanies it, and learn biblical concepts like "faith" and "holiness" found in its lyrics.

The songs are arranged in easy-to-sing keys. The melodies focus on unison parts with occasional harmonies. Full-color illustrations reinforce biblical contexts and background. Perfect for children's choir programs, Christian school and home school activities, and fun family sing-alongs!

Three companion products provide additional versatility. **The Kids Hymnal 3-CD Set** features all 80 songs recorded in split-track format and presented in corresponding page order to make singing along easier. **The Kids Hymnal DVD** allows you to project lyrics onscreen so everybody can participate. **The Kids Hymnal Piano Accompaniment Book** offers simple arrangements of piano scores and guitar chords for musicians to join in the performance.

Let's raise the bar in Christian music education and training! Let's sing about faith, about holiness, about joy, and about the wonders of God. Your kids will love—and learn a lot from—the time-honored hymns, Scripture songs, Sunday school favorites, and seasonal classics in **The Kids Hymnal**.

Stephen Elkins
Creative Director

Stephen Elkins's work has been nominated for the prestigious Grammy Award, and his Christian education products have sold over 10 million copies.

1 Amazing Grace

John Newton
John Rees

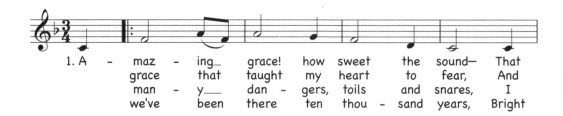

1. A - maz - ing__ grace! how sweet the sound— That
   grace that taught my heart to fear, And
   man - y__ dan - gers, toils and snares, I
   we've been there ten thou - sand years, Bright

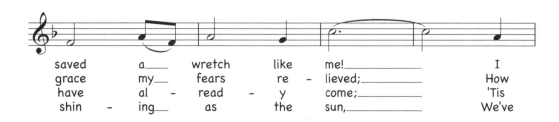

saved a__ wretch like me!_____ I
grace my__ fears re - lieved;_____ How
have al - read - y come;_____ 'Tis
shin - ing__ as the sun,_____ We've

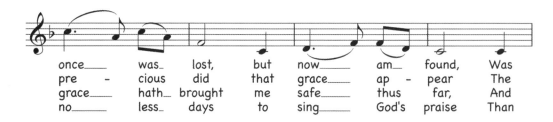

once____ was__ lost, but now____ am__ found, Was
pre - cious did that grace____ ap - pear The
grace____ hath__ brought me safe____ thus far, And
no____ less__ days to sing____ God's praise Than

| 1.2.3. | | 4. |

blind but__ now I see._____ 2. 'Twas ____
hour I__ first be - lieved._____ 3. Through
grace will__ lead me home._____ 4. When
when we'd__ first be - gun._____

The Reason We Sing:

Grace means undeserved favor. We did nothing to earn our forgiveness. We did nothing to deserve God's favor. It is a gift given by God to those who receive his Son as Lord and Savior. And it truly is amazing. He reaches out in love, offering grace to anyone who will receive it. The gift is free but not without cost. Jesus died on a cross so that we might receive God's grace!

MY AFFIRMATION:

I will receive God's grace.

2 Be Thou My Vision

Eleanor Hull
Traditional Irish Hymn

1. Be Thou my Vi - sion, O Lord of my heart;
2. Be Thou my Wis - dom, and Thou my true Word;
3. Rich - es I heed not, nor man's emp - ty praise,
4. High King of heav - en, my vic - to - ry won,

Naught be all else to me, save that Thou art—
I ev - er with Thee and Thou with me, Lord;
Thou mine in - her - it - ance, now and al - ways;
May I reach heav - en's joys O bright heav'n's Sun!

Thou my best thought, by day or by night,
Thou my great Fa - ther, I Thy true son,
Thou and Thou on - ly, first in my heart,
Heart of my own heart, what - ev - er be - fall,

Wak - ing or sleep - ing, Thy pres - ence my
Thou in me dwell - ing, and I with Thee
High King of heav - en, my Trea - sure Thou
Still be my Vi - sion, O Rul - er of

1.2.3.
light.
one.
art.

4. opt. upper harm.
all.

The Reason We Sing:

Vision means sight. When we have vision, we are able to see where we are going. Vision also allows us to see danger in our path. This hymn is actually a prayer asking the Lord to help us see the right way to live.

MY AFFIRMATION:

I will ask God to help me
see the right way to go!

3 When the Roll Is Called Up Yonder

James Black

With a triplet feel

1. When   the   trum - pet   of   the   Lord   shall   sound   and
2. On   that   bright   and   cloud - less   morn - ing   when   the
3. Let   us   la - bor   for   the   Mas - ter   from   the

time shall   be   no more   And   the   morn-ing   breaks   e - ter - nal   bright and
dead   in Christ shall rise   And   the   glo - ry   of   His   res - ur - rec - tion
dawn till   set - ting sun,   Let   us   talk   of   all   His   won -drous love   and

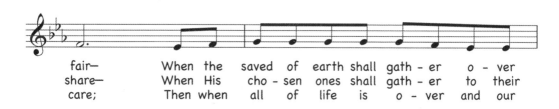

fair—   When   the   saved   of   earth shall   gath - er   o - ver
share—   When His   cho - sen   ones shall   gath - er   to   their
care;   Then when   all   of   life   is   o - ver   and   our

on   the oth - er shore   And   the   roll   is   called   up   yon - der,   I'll   be
home be - yond the skies   And   the   roll   is   called   up   yon - der,   I'll   be
work   on earth   is   done   And   the   roll   is   called   up   yon - der,   I'll   be

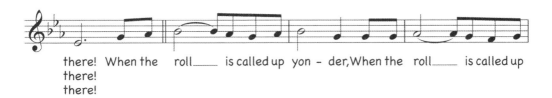

there! When the roll_____ is called up yon - der, When the roll_____ is called up
there!
there!

yon - der, When the roll_____ is called up yon - der—When the

roll is called up yon-der I'll be there!   there!

The Reason We Sing:

When your teacher "calls the roll," she is checking the names on her list to see who is there. The Bible says that one day, God will have a roll call. He is going to open a very special book in heaven called The Lamb's Book of Life. Everyone whose name is written in this book will enter the kingdom of heaven.

MY AFFIRMATION:

I want my name to be in the Lamb's Book of Life!

4 The Old Rugged Cross

George Bennard

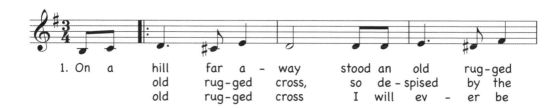

1. On a hill far a - way stood an old rug-ged
   old rug-ged cross, so de - spised by the
   old rug-ged cross I will ev - er be

cross, The em - blem of suf - f'ring and shame. And I
world, Has a won - drous at - trac - tion for me; For the
true, its shame and re - proach glad - ly bear; Then He'll

love that old cross where the dear - est and best For a
dear Lamb of God left His glo - ry a - bove To
call me some day to my home far a - way, Where His

world of lost sin - ners was slain. So I'll
bear it to dark Cal - va - ry.
glo - ry for - ev - er I'll share.

cher - ish the old rug-ged cross,_____ 'Till my tro - phies at

last I lay down;_____ I will cling to the old rug-ged cross,_____ And ex-

change it some day for a crown.

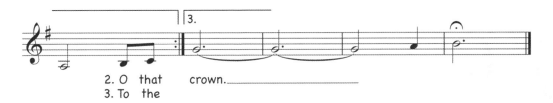

2. O that crown._____
3. To the

The Reason We Sing:

Jesus referred to the cross many times throughout His earthly ministry. In fact, He used it to teach us what it means to follow Him. He said, "First you must deny yourself." This means we don't do things for selfish reasons. Next we must "take up our cross," which means embrace the ministry that God desires for you. Then, we follow Jesus … wherever He leads.

> **MY AFFIRMATION:**
> ## I will follow Jesus!

5 Holy, Holy, Holy

Reginald Heber
John B. Dykes

1. Ho - ly, ho - ly, ho - ly! Lord___ God Al - might - y!
2. Ho - ly, ho - ly, ho - ly! all the saints a - dore Thee,
3. Ho - ly, ho - ly, ho - ly! though the dark-ness hide Thee,
4. Ho - ly, ho - ly, ho - ly! Lord___ God Al - might - y!

Ear - ly in the morn - ing our song shall rise to
Cast - ing down their gold - en crowns a - round the glass - y
Though the eye of sin - ful man Thy glo - ry may not
All Thy works shall praise Thy name in earth and sky and

Thee; Ho - ly, ho - ly, ho - ly! mer - ci - ful and
sea; Cher - u - bim and ser - a - phim fall - ing down be -
see; On - ly Thou art ho - ly— there is none be -
sea; Ho - ly, ho - ly, ho - ly! mer - ci - ful and

might - y! God in three Per - sons, bless - ed Trin - i -
fore Thee, Which wert and art and ev - er - more shalt
side Thee, Per - fect in pow'r, in love and pur - i -
might - y! God in three Per - sons, bless - ed Trin - i -

1.2.3.

ty!
be.
ty.

4.

ty!

The Reason We Sing:

To be holy is to be without sin and set apart. In Revelation 4:8, the angels in heaven sing, "Holy, holy, holy, Lord God Almighty!" God is being worshipped as the one true God, perfect and holy in every way. With God's help, we, too, can live a life of holiness, a life set apart for God's service.

MY AFFIRMATION:
I will try to be holy!

6 Come, Christians, Join to Sing

Christian Bateman
Spanish Melody

1. Come, Chris-tians, join to sing Al - le - lu - ia!
2. Come, lift your hearts on high, Al - le - lu - ia!
3. Praise yet our Christ a - gain, Al - le - lu - ia!

A - men! Loud praise to Christ our King;
A - men! Let prais - es fill the sky;
A - men! Life shall not end the strain;

Al - le - lu - ia! A - men! Let all, with
Al - le - lu - ia! A - men! He is our
Al - le - lu - ia! A - men! On heav - en's

heart and voice, Be - fore His throne re - joice; Praise is His
Guide and Friend; To us He'll con - de- scend; His love shall
bliss - ful shore His good - ness we'll a - dore, Sing - ing for -

gra - cious choice: Al - le - lu - ia! A - men!
nev - er end: Al - le - lu - ia! A - men!
ev - er - more, "Al - le - lu - ia! A - men!"

1.2. 3.

The Reason We Sing:

What does it mean to be a Christian? It means that all our sins are forgiven and forgotten. In this world, we may have momentary troubles. But rejoice and sing … heaven awaits us. That gives us a reason to sing!

MY AFFIRMATION:
I will sing to the Lord!

7 Blessed Assurance

Fanny Crosby
Phoebe Knapp

1. Bless-ed as - sur - ance, Je - sus is mine!_____
2. Per-fect sub - mis - sion, per-fect de - light!_____
3. Per-fect sub - mis - sion— all is at rest,_____

O what a fore - taste of glo - ry di - vine!_____
Vi - sions of rap - ture now burst on my sight;_____
I in my Sav - ior am hap - py and blest;_____

Heir of sal - va - tion, pur-chase of God,_____
An - gels de - scend - ing bring from a - bove._____
Watch-ing and wait - ing, look - ing a - bove,_____

Born of His Spir - it, washed in His blood._____
Ech - oes of mer - cy, whis - pers of love._____
Filled with His good - ness, lost in His love._____

This is my sto - ry, this is my song._____ Prais-ing my

Sav - ior all the day long;_____ This is my sto - ry,

this is my song,_____ Prais-ing my Sav - ior all the day

1.2. long.

3. long.

MY AFFIRMATION:

Jesus is mine!

15

8 Standing on the Promises

Kelso Carter

with a triplet feel

1. Stand-ing on the prom -is - es of Christ my King,
2. Stand-ing on the prom -is - es that can - not fail,
3. Stand-ing on the prom -is - es of Christ the Lord,
4. Stand-ing on the prom - is - es I can - not fall,

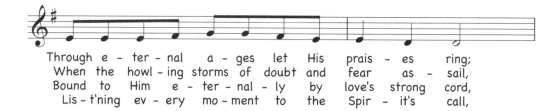

Through e - ter - nal a - ges let His prais - es ring;
When the howl - ing storms of doubt and fear as - sail,
Bound to Him e - ter - nal - ly by love's strong cord,
Lis - t'ning ev - ery mo - ment to the Spir - it's call,

Glo - ry in the high - est I will shout and sing,
By the liv - ing Word of God I shall pre - vail,
O - ver - com - ing dai - ly with the Spir - it's sword,
Rest - ing in my Sav - ior as my all in all,

Stand-ing on the pro - mis - es of God. Stand - ing,

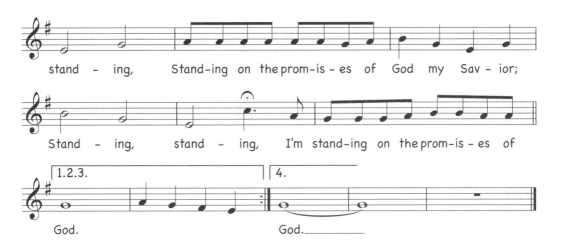

stand - ing, Stand-ing on the prom-is - es of God my Sav - ior;

Stand - ing, stand - ing, I'm stand-ing on the prom-is - es of

1.2.3. God.

4. God.

The Reason We Sing:

We can stand on many different things. We can stand on a ladder. It becomes our support. As we walk across a room, the floor supports the weight of our bodies. But what can support the weight of sin? The weight of troubles? The promises of God! We can stand on the promises of God found in the Bible.

MY AFFIRMATION:
I will stand on God's promises!

9 Fairest Lord Jesus

Schlesische Volkslieder

1. Fair - est Lord Je - sus, Rul - er of all na - ture,
2. Fair are the mead - ows, Fair - er still the wood - lands,
3. Fair is the sun - shine, Fair - er still the moon - light,
4. Beau - ti - ful Sav - ior! Lord of the na - tions!

O Thou of God and man the Son: Thee will I
Robed in the bloom - ing garb of spring; Je - sus is
And all the twin - kling star - ry host; Je - sus shines
Son of God and Son of Man! Glo - ry and

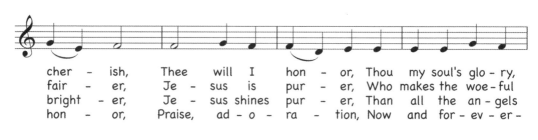

cher - ish, Thee will I hon - or, Thou my soul's glo - ry,
fair - er, Je - sus is pur - er, Who makes the woe - ful
bright - er, Je - sus shines pur - er, Than all the an - gels
hon - or, Praise, ad - o - ra - tion, Now and for - ev - er -

opt. upper harm. last time | 1.2.3. | 4.

joy, and crown. Thine!
heart to sing.
heav'n can boast.
more be

The Reason We Sing:

This hymn declares Jesus to be fairer than anything we may see in nature. More beautiful than the meadows, the woodlands, or the most spectacular sunrise … Jesus outshines them all! And it is the love of Jesus that makes Him the fairest of them all!

MY AFFIRMATION:
Jesus is ruler of everything!

10 Near the Cross

Fanny Crosby
William Doane

1. Je - sus, keep my near the cross— There a
2. Near the cross, a trem - bling soul, Love and
3. Near the cross I'll watch and wait, Hop - ing,

pre - cious foun - tain, Free to all, a
mer - cy found me; There the Bright and
trust - ing ev - er, Till I reach the

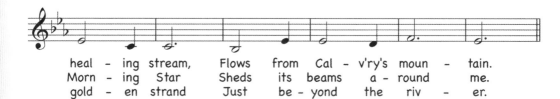

heal - ing stream, Flows from Cal - v'ry's moun - tain.
Morn - ing Star Sheds its beams a - round me.
gold - en strand Just be - yond the riv - er.

In the cross, in the cross

Be my glo - ry ev - er, 'Till my rap - tured

soul   shall   find   Rest,   be - yond   the   riv -

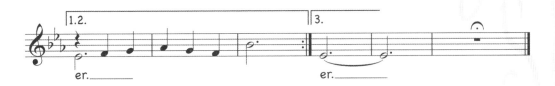

er.____   er.____

The Reason We Sing:

We should live in the light of the cross. What Jesus has done for us should never be forgotten. Because of His sacrifice, our sins are forgiven.

MY AFFIRMATION:

I will live in the light of the cross!

11 Count Your Blessings

Johnson Oatman Jr.
Edwin O. Excell

1. When up - on life's bil - lows you are tem - pest tossed,
2. Are you ev - er bur-dened with a load of care?
3. So, a - mid the con - flict, wheth - er great or small,

When you are dis - cour-aged, think - ing all is lost,
Does the cross seem heav - y you are called to bear?
Do not be dis - cour-aged, God is o - ver all;

Count your man - y bless - ings, name them one by one,
Count your man - y bless - ings, eve - ry doubt will fly,
Count your man - y bless - ings, an - gels will at - tend,

And it will sur - prise you what the Lord hath done.
And you will be sing - ing as the days go by.
Help and com - fort give you to your jour - ney's end.

Count   your bless-ings, Name them one   by   one;   Count   your

bless-ings, See what God   hath   done.   Count   your bless-ings,

Name them one   by   one;   Count your man-y   bless-ings, See what

1.2.
God hath   done._____

3.
done.

The Reason We Sing:

Our lives are so full of blessings! Some blessings are very big, others are small. We have plenty of food to eat and clothes to wear. Our homes are warm and our pillows are soft. Let's remember to be thankful and count our blessings.

MY AFFIRMATION:
I will be thankful!

23

12 When We All Get to Heaven

Eliza Hewitt
Emily Wilson

Let us sing.

1. Sing the won - drous love of Je - sus,
2. While we walk the pil - grim path-way

Sing His mer - cy and His grace; In the man - sions
Clouds will o - ver - spead the sky; But when trav - 'ling

bright and bless - ed He'll pre - pare for us a place. When we
days are o - ver, Not a shad - ow, not a sigh.

all get to heav - en What a day of re - joic - ing that will

be! When we all see Je - sus, We'll

1.

sing and shout the vic - to - ry. Let us

2.

ry; We'll sing and shout the vic - to - ry.

Let us sing, Let us sing.____

The Reason We Sing:

It is always exciting to move from one place to another. Everything is new! You may have a new school, a new church and even a new home. The Bible says that one day, we all are going to move. Christians will go to be with Jesus in heaven and live with Him there!

MY AFFIRMATION:

Jesus is all the world to me!

13 O How I Love Jesus

Frederick Whitfield

1. There is a name__ I love to hear, I
   tells me of__ a Sav - ior's love, who
   tells me what__ my Fa - ther hath In
   tells of One__ whose lov - ing heart Can

love to sing__ its worth;_____ It
died to set__ me free;_____ It
store for ev - ery day,_____ And,
feel my deep - est woe,_____ Who

sounds like mu - sic in my ear, The
tells me of__ His pre - cious blood, The
though I tread__ a dark - some path, Yields
in each sor - row bears a part That

sweet - est name on earth._____
sin - ner's per - fect plea._____
sun - shine all the way._____
none__ can bear be - low._____

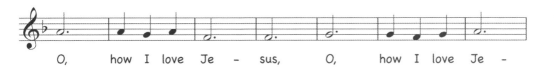

O, how I love Je - sus, O, how I love Je -

sus,_____ O, how I love Je - sus— Be - cause__ He

first loved me!

2. It
3. It
4. It

The Reason We Sing:

Before you ever heard the name "Jesus," His love was reaching out for you. He was there walking beside you, helping you grow up. And then one day, you heard His name. Maybe at church, or at home; maybe a friend told you. And you discovered this wonderful truth: We love Him because He first loved us!

MY AFFIRMATION:

I love Jesus because He loves me!

14 What a Friend We Have in Jesus

Joseph Scriven
Charles Converse

1. What a Friend we have in Je - sus, All our sins and griefs to
2. Have we tri - als and temp - ta - tions? Is there trou - ble an - y -
3. Are we weak and heav - y - la - den, Cum - bered with a load of

bear! What a priv - i - lege to car - ry
where? We should nev - er be dis - cour - aged,
care? Pre - cious Sav - ior, still our Ref - uge—

Eve - ry-thing to God in prayer! O what peace we of - ten
Take it to the Lord in prayer. Can we find a friend so
Take it to the Lord in prayer. Do thy friends des- pise, for-

for - feit, O what need-less pain we bear.
faith - ful Who will all our sor-rows share?
sake thee? Take it to the Lord in prayer;

All be-cause we do not car - ry Eve - ry-thing to God in
Je - sus knows our eve - ry weak - ness, Take it to the Lord in
In His arms He'll take and shield thee, Thou wilt find a sol - ace

prayer!
prayer.

there._____

The Reason We Sing:

It is really wonderful to have best friends. You can always count on a friend to be there in the good times and in the bad. That is why Jesus is the greatest friend of all. He's always there to help us in a time of trouble.

MY AFFIRMATION:

Jesus is my best friend!

15 I Have Decided to Follow Jesus

Anonymous

The Reason We Sing:

Have you ever followed a road which led to a dead end? It's not much fun going back when you could have decided on the right way to go. Jesus said, "I am the Way. No man comes to the Father except through me." There are no dead ends with Jesus! Following Him will lead us right into the arms of God our Father and a home in heaven.

MY AFFIRMATION:
I will follow Jesus!

Traditional Spiritual

1. He's got the whole_____ world_ in His hands, He's got the
   wind_ and the rain___ in His hands, He's got the
   ti-ny lit-tle ba-by in His hands, He's got the
   you and me__ broth-er, in His hands, He's got__

whole_____ world_ in His hands,_ He's got the
wind__ and the rain___ in His hands,_ He's got the
ti-ny lit-tle ba-by in His hands,_ He's got the
you and me___ sis-ter, in His hands,_ He's got__

whole_____ world_ in His hands,_ He's got the
wind__ and the rain___ in His hands,_
ti-ny lit-tle ba-by in His hands,_
you and me__ broth-er, in His hands,_

1.2.3.

whole world in His hands.__

4.

2. He's got the _____
3. He's got the
4. He's got__

The Reason We Sing:

The world is a very big place. Yet all that is in this world was created by our mighty God. And not a sparrow falls to the ground without Him knowing about it. Being "in God's hands" means that we are in His care. Yes, God cares for you!

MY AFFIRMATION:

I know God cares for me!

17 All Creatures of Our God and King

St. Francis
William Draper

1. All crea-tures of our God and King, Lift
rush-ing wind that art so strong, Ye
all things their Cre-a-tor bless, And

up your voice and with us sing, Al - le -
clouds that sail in heav'n a - long, O_____
wor - ship Him in hum - ble - ness. O_____

lu - ia! Al - le - lu - ia! Thou
praise Him! Al - le - lu - ia! Thou
praise Him! Al - le - lu - ia! Praise,

burn - ing sun with gold - en beam, Thou
ris - ing morn, in praise re - joice, Ye
praise the Fa - ther, praise the Son, And

sil - ver moon with soft - er gleam,   O____ praise Him! O____
lights of eve - ning, find a voice!
praise the Spir - it, Three in One!

praise Him! Al - le - lu - ia! Al - le - lu - ia! Al - le - lu -

1.2.   **3.**
ia!   2. Thou ia!
                                             3. Let

The Reason We Sing:

Sometimes an artist will cover his new painting so that no one can see it. When the artist removes the covering, everyone applauds! God's creation is like that. At night, all is dark. The dark is like a covering over all God has made; then comes the sunrise. We see the sun, the light, and the incredible colors. All that God made is revealed, and we applaud! That's called praise ... we praise the Lord!

18 Joyful, Joyful, We Adore Thee

Harry van Dyke
Ludwig van Beethoven

1. Joy - ful, joy - ful, we a - dore Thee, God of glo - ry,
2. All Thy works with joy sur - round Thee, Earth and heav'n re -
3. Thou art giv - ing and for - giv - ing, Ev - er bless - ing,
4. Mor - tals, join the hap - py cho - rus Which the morn - ing

Lord of love; Hearts un - fold like flow'rs be - fore Thee,
flect Thy rays, Stars and an - gels sing a - round Thee,
ev - er blest, Well-spring of the joy of liv - ing,
stars be - gan; Fa - ther love is reign - ing o'er us,

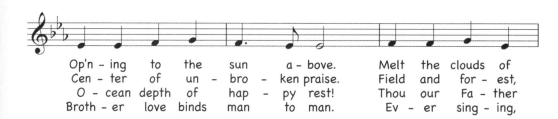

Op'n - ing to the sun a - bove. Melt the clouds of
Cen - ter of un - bro - ken praise. Field and for - est,
O - cean depth of hap - py rest! Thou our Fa - ther
Broth - er love binds man to man. Ev - er sing - ing,

sin and sad - ness, Drive the dark of doubt a - way;
vale and moun - tain, Flow - 'ry mea - dow, flash - ing sea,
Christ, our Broth - er— All who live in love are Thine;
march we on - ward, Vic - tors in the midst of strife,

Giv - er   of   im - mor - tal glad - ness, Fill us with the
Chant - ing bird and flow - ing foun - tain, Call us to   re -
Teach us how to   love each oth - er,   Lift us to   the
Joy - ful mu - sic leads us sun - ward In   the tri - umph

1.2.3.   **4.**

light of day.   song of life.____
joice in Thee.
joy di - vine.

The Reason We Sing:

Do you know the difference between joy and happiness? Happiness comes and goes. It depends on where we are and what is happening around us. But joy is here to stay. It comes from knowing God. The Bible says "The joy of the Lord is my strength." So no matter where you are or what is happening, the joy of the Lord is your strength!

MY AFFIRMATION:

God brings me joy!

19 *O Happy Day*

Philip Doddridge
Edward Rimbault

1. O hap - py day that fixed my choice On Thee, my
bond that seals my vows To Him who
great trans - ac - tion's done— I am the
long - di - vid - ed heart, Fixed on this

Sav - ior and my God! Well may this glow - ing heart re -
mer - its all my love! Let cheer-ful an - thems fill His
Lord's and He is mine; He drew me, and I fol-lowed
bliss - ful cen - ter, rest, Nor ev - er from my Lord de -

opt. lower harm.

joice And tell its rap - tures all a - broad. Hap - py
house, While to that sa - cred shrine I move.
on, Charmed to con - fess the voice di - vine.
part, With Him of ev - ery good pos - sessed.

day, hap - py day, When Je - sus washed my sins a - way! He taught me

how to watch and pray And live re - joic - ing eve - ry day; Hap-py

1.2.3.

day, hap - py day, When Je - sus washed my sins a - way!

4.

2. O hap - py way!_____
3. 'Tis done, the
4. Now rest, my

The Reason We Sing:

To rejoice is to celebrate. On your birthday, you rejoiced to receive all those presents! The same is true with the Lord. We rejoice that we have received His salvation. We rejoice that we receive His promises to love us, to keep us, and bless us. We celebrate the blessing of knowing and loving a wonderful God.

MY AFFIRMATION:

I will rejoice for what God has done!

20 Leaning on the Everlasting Arms

Elisha Hoffram
Anthony Showalter

with a triplet feel

1. What a fel-low-ship, what a joy di-vine, Lean-ing on the ev-er-
2. O how sweet to walk in this pil-grim way, Lean-ing on the ev-er-
3. What have I to dread, what have I to fear, Lean-ing on the ev-er-

last-ing arms; What a bless-ed-ness, what a peace is mine,
last-ing arms; O, how bright the path grows from day to day,
last-ing arms; I have bless-ed peace with my Lord so near,

Lean-ing on the ev-er-last-ing arms. Lean - ing, lean - ing,
Lean-ing on the ev-er-last-ing arms.
Lean-ing on the ev-er-last-ing arms.

Safe and se-cure from all a-larms; Lean - ing,

1.2.

lean - ing, Lean-ing on the ev-er-last-ing arms.

3.

last-ing arms.

The Reason We Sing:

To lean on others is to depend on their ability or strength. They are holding you up! It's like leaning on a wall. The Bible says, "Don't lean on your own understanding." That means we don't depend on what we know, but we "lean on the Lord," Let Him be your strength. Let His ability to part a sea and calm a storm bring you comfort!

MY AFFIRMATION:

I will depend on the Lord!

21 At the Cross

Isaac Watts
Ralph Hudson

1. A - las! and did my Sav - ior bleed? And did my Sov-'reign
   it for crimes that I have done, He suf-fered on the
   might the sun in dark - ness hide And shut His glo - ries
   drops of grief can ne'er re - pay The debt of love I

die? Would He de - vote that sa - cred head For
tree? A - maz - ing pit - y! grace un - known! And
in, When Christ, the might - y Mak - er, died For
owe: Here, Lord, I give my - self a - way, 'Tis

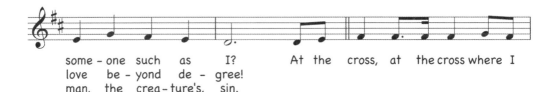

some - one such as I? At the cross, at the cross where I
love be - yond de - gree!
man, the crea - ture's, sin.
all that I can do!

first_ saw the light And the bur - den of my heart rolled a way, It was

there by faith I re-ceived my___ sight, And now I am hap-py all the

1.2.3.		4.

day!   day!

2. Was
3. Well
4. But

The Reason We Sing:

I once heard someone say, "I've been too bad to go to church. God wouldn't want me there." How untrue this is! God isn't looking for perfect people to come to church. He's looking for sinners that want to change. The church isn't full of perfect people … it's full of people made perfect by the cross of Christ.

MY AFFIRMATION:

I will come to the cross!

22 Stand Up, Stand Up for Jesus

George Duffield, Jr.
George Webb

1. Stand up, stand up for Je - sus, Ye sol - diers of the cross, Lift
up, stand up for Je - sus, The trum - pet call o - bey; Forth
up, stand up for Je - sus, Stand in His strength a - lone; The
up, stand up for Je - sus, The strife will not be long; This

high His roy - al ban - ner, It must not suf - fer loss; From
to the might - y con - flict In this His glo - rious day, Ye
arm of flesh will fail you— Ye dare not trust your own; Put
day the noise of bat - tle, The next, the vic - tor's song; To

vic - tory un - to vic - tory His ar - my shall He lead,_____ 'Till
that are men, now serve Him A - gainst un - num - bered foes;_____ Let
on the gos - pel ar - mor, Each piece put on with prayer;_____ Where
him who o - ver - com - eth A crown of life shall be;_____ He

eve - ry foe is van - quished And Christ is Lord in -
cour - age rise with dan - ger, And strength to strength op -
du - ty calls, or dan - ger, Be nev - er want - ing
with the King of glo - ry Shall reign e - ter - nal -

1.2.3. | 4.

deed._____   2. Stand   ly.
pose._____   3. Stand
there._____   4. Stand

The Reason We Sing:

The General stood before his soldiers and shouted, "If you're with us, stand up and be counted!" The brave men stood up. They wanted their General to know they were ready to go to battle. Christians are like that. God calls us to stand up in this world. We shouldn't be ashamed or afraid to stand up and fight for Him!

MY AFFIRMATION:
I will stand up for Jesus!

23 Crown Him with Many Crowns

Matthew Bridges
Godfrey Thring
George Elfey

1. Crown Him with man - y crowns, The Lamb up - on His
2. Crown Him the Lord of love: Be - hold His hands and
3. Crown Him the Lord of life: Who tri - umphed o'er the
4. Crown Him the Lord of heav'n: One with the Fa - ther

throne; Hark! how the heav'n - ly an - them__ drowns All
side— Rich wounds, yet vis - i - ble a - bove, In
grave, who rose vic - to - rious to the__ strife For
known, One with the Spir - it through Him__ giv'n From

mu - sic but its own! A - wake, my soul and
beau - ty glo - ri - fied. No an - gel in the
those He came to save. His glo - ries now we
yon - der glo - rious throne. To Thee be end - less

sing Of Him who died for thee, And
sky Can ful - ly bear that sight, But
sing, Who died and rose on high, Who
praise, For Thou for us hast died; Be

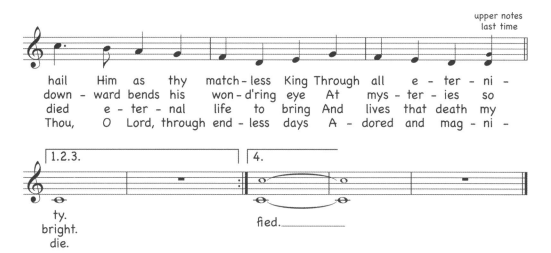

upper notes
last time

hail	Him	as	thy	match-less	King	Through	all	e - ter - ni -
down - ward	bends	his	won-d'ring	eye	At	mys - ter - ies	so
died	e - ter - nal	life	to	bring	And	lives	that	death	my
Thou,	O	Lord,	through	end - less	days	A -	dored	and	mag - ni -

1.2.3.

4.

ty.
bright.
die.

fied._____

The Reason We Sing:

Kings and queens wear a crown as a symbol of their authority. It shows they have the right to rule. In this hymn, Jesus is given a crown because of the sacrifice He made for us on the cross. We crown Him King of Kings and Lord of Lords, the ruler of our hearts.

MY AFFIRMATION:
I will make
Jesus the King
of my life!

47

24 For the Beauty of the Earth

Folliott Pierpoint
Conrad Kocher

1. For the beau - ty of the earth, For the glo - ry
2. For the won - der of each hour Of the day and
3. For Thy Church that ev - er - more Lift - eth ho - ly
4. For Thy - self, best gift di - vine, To our race so

of the skies, For the love which from our birth
of the night, Hill and vale and tree and flower,
hands a - bove. Off - 'ring up on eve - ry shore
free - ly giv'n; For that great, great love of Thine,

O - ver and a - round us lies; Lord of all, to
Sun and moon and stars of light;
Her pure sac - ri - fice of love.
Peace on earth and joy in heav'n.

1.2.3.

Thee we raise This our hymn of grate - ful praise.

4.

grate - ful praise.

The Reason We Sing:

King David wrote, "The heavens declare the glory of God and the skies proclaim the work of His hands." He saw the beauty of God in the petals of a rose. He saw the majesty of God in the snow-capped mountains. And he saw God's awesome power in the rushing waters. David praised God for the beauty of the earth.

MY AFFIRMATION:
I praise God for His creation!

25 How Great Thou Art

Stuart K. Hine

1. O Lord my God, when I in awe - some
   woods and for - est glades I
   think that God, His Son not
   come with shout of ac - cla -

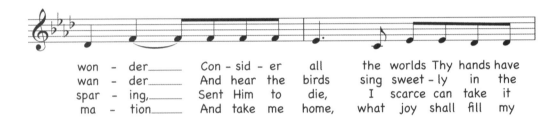

won - der_____ Con - sid - er all the worlds Thy hands have
wan - der_____ And hear the birds sing sweet - ly in the
spar - ing,_____ Sent Him to die, I scarce can take it
ma - tion_____ And take me home, what joy shall fill my

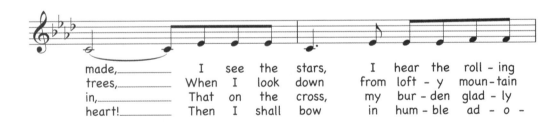

made,_____ I see the stars, I hear the roll - ing
trees,_____ When I look down from loft - y moun - tain
in,_____ That on the cross, my bur - den glad - ly
heart! Then I shall bow in hum - ble ad - o -

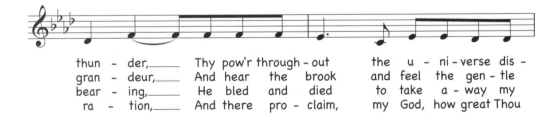

thun - der,_____ Thy pow'r through - out the u - ni - verse dis -
gran - deur,_____ And hear the brook and feel the gen - tle
bear - ing,_____ He bled and died to take a - way my
ra - tion,_____ And there pro - claim, my God, how great Thou

played.___ Then sings my   soul,   my Sav - ior God, to   Thee;___ How great Thou
breeze.___
sin.___
art.___

art,___ how great Thou art!___ Then sings my   soul,   my Sav - ior God, to

Thee:___ How great Thou   art,___ how great Thou   art!

1.2.3.

4.

2. When   through the   art!___
3. And   when   I
4. When   Christ shall

The Reason We Sing:

The psalmist wrote, "Great is the Lord and worthy of praise." His greatness lies in the fact that He has done what no other can do. He has created this world full of incredible living things. He sustains His creation day by day so that nothing happens without His knowledge. Most importantly, He has redeemed mankind with the blood of His own son, Jesus Christ. Yes, great is the Lord ... for He creates, He sustains, and He redeems this world!

26 God Will Take Care of You

Civilla Martin
Stillman Martin

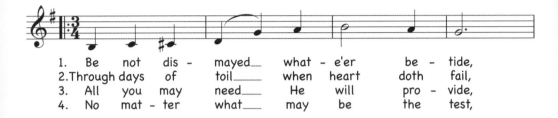

1. Be not dis - mayed___ what - e'er be - tide,
2. Through days of toil___ when heart doth fail,
3. All you may need___ He will pro - vide,
4. No mat - ter what___ may be the test,

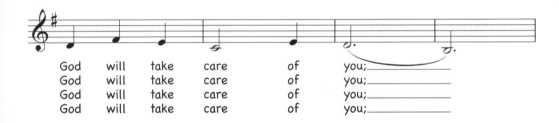

God will take care of you;___
God will take care of you;___
God will take care of you;___
God will take care of you;___

Be - neath His wings___ of love a - bide,
When dan - gers fierce___ your path as - sail,
Noth - ing you ask___ will be de - nied,
Lean, wea - ry one,___ up - on His breast,

God will take care of you.___
God will take care of you.___
God will take care of you.___
God will take care of you.___

opt. lower harm.

God will take care of you, Through eve - ry day,

o'er all the way; He will take care__ of you,

1.2.3.

4.

God will take care__ of you._____ you._____

The Reason We Sing:

Who is Lord of your life? Do you seek to please God by trusting and obeying his word? Then He is Lord! Or, do you seek to please yourself, regardless of what the Bible says? Then, sadly, you are lord ... and that's not good. God should always come first in your life. He is Lord indeed!

MY AFFIRMATION:

I will seek to please God because He is Lord!

27 He Keeps Me Singing as I Go

Luther Bridgers

1. There's with-in my heart a mel-o-dy— Je-sus whis-pers sweet and
2. Feast-ing on the rich-es of His grace, Rest-ing 'neath His shel-t'ring

low,_____ "Fear not, I am with thee— peace, be still,"
wing,_____ Al-ways look-ing on His smil-ing face—

In all of life's ebb and flow. Je-sus, Je-sus, Je-sus—
That is why I shout and sing.

Sweet-est name I know. Fills my eve-ry long-ing,

take Coda
3rd time
1.
Keeps me sing-ing as I go.

2. D.S. al Coda

go. go._____

The Reason We Sing:

There are days when we feel sad. That's okay! Everyone feels sad at one time or another. But we don't have to stay that way. Even though we may be having a bad day, we are not alone! Jesus is with us. And for that, we can be glad!

MY AFFIRMATION:

Jesus is with me!

28 Have Thine Own Way, Lord

Adelaide Pollard
George Stebbirs

1. Have Thine own way, Lord! Have Thine own way!
2. Have Thine own way, Lord! Have Thine own way!
3. Have Thine own way, Lord! Have Thine own way!
4. Have Thine own way, Lord! Have Thine own way!

Thou art the Pot - ter, I am the clay.
Search me and try me, Mas - ter, to - day!
Wound - ed and wea - ry, help me, I pray!
Hold o'er my be - ing ab - so - lute sway!

Mold me and make me af - ter Thy will, While I am wait -
Whit - er than snow, Lord, wash me just now, As in thy pres -
Pow - er— all pow - er— sure - ly is Thine! Touch me and heal
Fill with Thy Spir - it till all shall see Christ on - ly, al -

1.2.3.

ing, yield - ed and still.
ence hum - bly I bow.
me, Sav - ior di - vine!
ways, liv - ing in

4.

me!

The Reason We Sing:

Once we give our hearts to Jesus, a process begins. We are like a lump of clay resting on the potter's wheel. The potter is a person who makes things out of clay by turning the clay on a wheel. Like a potter, God begins to mold us into what He wants us to be. He begins to shape our lives so that we begin to be more like Jesus.

MY AFFIRMATION:

I am becoming more like Jesus!

29 This Is My Father's World

Maltbie Babcock
Franklin Sheppard

1. This__ is my Fa-ther's world, And__ to my lis-tening
   is my Fa-ther's world, The__ birds their car-ols
   is my Fa-ther's world, O__ let me ne'er for-

ears   All   na-ture sings, and__ round me rings The
raise, The   morn-ing light, the__ lil-y white, De-
get   That though the wrong seems. oft so strong, God

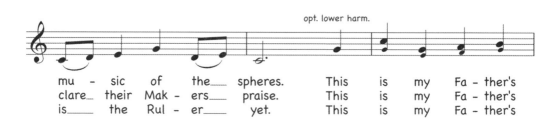

opt. lower harm.

mu-sic of the__ spheres.   This is my Fa-ther's
clare_ their Mak-ers__ praise.   This is my Fa-ther's
is__ the Rul-er__ yet.   This is my Fa-ther's

world: I__ rest me in the thought   Of__
world: He__ shines in all that's fair;   In the
world: The__ bat-tle is not done;   Je-

rocks and trees, of___ skies and seas— His hand___ the won - ders___
rus - tling grass I___ hear Him pass, He speaks___ to me eve-ry -
sus who died shall be sat - is - fied, And earth___ and heav'n be___

1.2. **3.**

wrought!
where.   2. This___ one.___
one.   3. This___

The Reason We Sing:

Did you ever look up at the stars at night and wonder how this world came to be? Some say it just happened. Christians say it happened for a reason. And that reason is God! Genesis 1:1 says "In the beginning God created the heavens and the earth." How did He do it? With His Words! God spoke and all things came to be. We have a mighty Father...and this is truly our Father's world!

MY AFFIRMATION:
God our Father created all things!

30 Come, Thou Almighty King

Felice de Giardini
Italian Hymn

1. Come, Thou Al - might - y King, Help us Thy
2. Come, Thou In - car - nate Word, Gird on Thy
3. Come, Ho - ly Com - fort - er, Thy sa - cred
4. To Thee, great One in Three, E - ter - nal

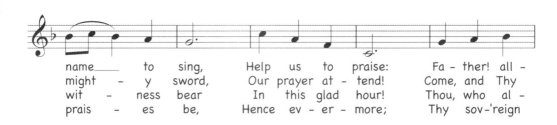

name to sing, Help us to praise: Fa - ther! all -
might - y sword, Our prayer at - tend! Come, and Thy
wit - ness bear In this glad hour! Thou, who al -
prais - es be, Hence ev - er - more; Thy sov-'reign

glo - ri - ous, O'er all vic - to - ri - ous, Come, and reign
peo - ple bless, And give Thy word suc - cess; Spir - it of
might - y art, Now rule in ev - ery heart And ne'er from
maj - es - ty May we in glo - ry see, And to e -

opt. upper harm. last time
Fine last time
D.C.

o - ver us, An - cient of Days.
ho - li - ness, On us de - scend.
us de - part, Spir - it of pow'r.
ter - ni - ty Love and a - dore.

The Reason We Sing:

We serve a very real God. He sees us in our time of trouble. He rejoices with us when times are good. He listens to our prayers. His presence is with us no matter where we go. So we ask Him to come. Come and be near to us every single day!

MY AFFIRMATION:
I know God is near!

31 Jesus Loves Me

Anna Warner
William Bradbury

1. Je - sus loves me! this I know,   For the Bi - ble tells me so;
2. Je - sus loves me! He who died   Heav-en's gate to o - pen wide;
3. Je - sus loves me! He will stay   Close be-side me all the way;

Lit - tle ones to Him be-long,   They are weak but He is strong.
He will wash a - way my sin,   Let His lit - tle child come in.
Thou hast bled and died for me,   I will hence-forth live for Thee.

Yes, Je - sus loves me!   Yes, Je - sus loves me!   Yes, Je - sus

loves me! The Bi - ble tells me so.   so.

The Reason We Sing:

It is by faith that we believe Jesus loves us. Our faith is anchored in the Bible. The Bible says that Jesus showed us this love by laying down His life for us. He took the sins of the whole world upon Himself when He went to the cross. That is why I know "Jesus Loves Me!"

MY AFFIRMATION:

I know Jesus loves me!

32 The Mustard Seed

Stephen Elkins

In a "2" feel

If you have faith as small as a mus-tard seed, If you

have faith as small as a mus-tard seed, You can say to this moun-tain,

"Move from here to there!" And it will move, and it will move, and

it will move, and it will move, And noth-ing will be im - pos - si - ble for

you. Show a lit-tle faith my friend, watch the mir-a-cles be-

gin;

1. Moun - tains move, moun-tains move, O - ceans part,
2. Blind men see, blind men see, Thou-sands fed,
3. Moun - tains move, moun-tains move, O - ceans part,

o - ceans part with a Word of faith from a faith - ful_ heart and
thou-sands fed with_ Two small fish and_ sev -en loaves of bread and
o - ceans part with a Word of faith from a faith - ful_ heart and

Noth-ing will be im - pos - si - ble_ for you.
Noth-ing will be im - pos - si - ble_ for you.
Noth-ing will be im - poss - si - ble_ for you.

|1.2.

|3.

If you have faith as small as a mus-tard seed.

The Reason We Sing:

I saw a mountain that had been moved so that a road could go through it! And I thought of Jesus' words, "If you have faith as small as a mustard seed, you can say to this mountain, 'Move!', and it will move." Seeing that men can use trucks and shovels to move an entire mountain makes it easy to believe that faith can move any mountain that stands in my way!

MY AFFIRMATION:

I can move mountains
with just a little faith!

33 You Must Be Born Again

Stephen Elkins

1. Hear this song, come sing a - long, loud and strong, You must be born a - gain. Oh, the words you hear ring - ing in your ear Loud and clear; "You must be born a - gain."
2. Tell your friends His love be - gins and nev - er ends When you are born a - gain. Oh, there's just one way to heav - en's gate. Don't hes - i - tate, You must be born a - gain.

You must be born a - gain to have e - ter - nal life.

You must be born a-gain and live for Je - sus Christ.

Hear this__ song,__ come sing a - long,__ so
Tell your__ friends__ His love be - gins.__ and

loud and__ strong, "You must be born__ a - gain."__
nev - er__ ends,__ You must be born__ a - gain.__

Hear this__ song,__ come sing a - long,__ so
Tell your__ friends__ His love be - gins.__ and

1.
2.

loud and__strong,__ "You must be born__ a-gain."__ born__ a-gain.
nev- er__ ends,__ You must be

| **MY AFFIRMATION:** |
I have been born again!

34 Do to Others

Stephen Elkins

Do, do, do, do, do, do,___ do, do to oth-ers.___

Do, do, do, do, do, do,___ do, do to oth-ers.___

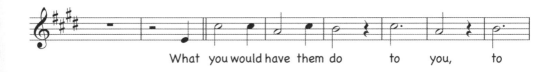

What you would have them do to you, to

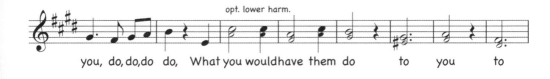

you, do, do, do do, What you would have them do to you to

You, Do, do, do, do, do,___ do, do to oth-ers.___

1st time D.C
2nd time go on
opt. upper harm.

1. If you want peo-ple to treat you nice, treat them nice, That's how it goes! If you want peo-ple to treat you nice, treat them nice, I say.___ Do, do, do, do, do, do,___ do, do to oth-ers.___ Do, do, do, do, do, do,___ do, do to oth-ers.___

2. If you want peo-ple to treat you kind, treat them kind, That's how it goes! If you want peo-ple to treat you kind, treat them kind, I say.___

MY AFFIRMATION:

I'll treat others the way
I'd like to be treated!

69

35 Do Not Judge

Stephen Elkins

in a swing "2" feel

Do not judge or you, too, will be judged.

Do not judge or you, too, will be judged.

For in that same way you judge oth-ers.

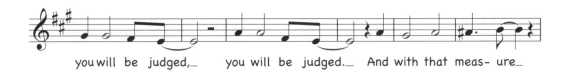

you will be judged, you will be judged. And with that meas-ure

you use to meas-ure it will be meas-ured un-to you.

The Reason We Sing:

It's called the Golden Rule. It's "golden" because of its great spiritual value. It teaches us to treat others the way that we would like to be treated. If you like it when someone helps you, then you help someone else. If you enjoy hearing a kind word, speak a kind word to someone else.

MY AFFIRMATION:

I will not
judge others!

36 I Am the Way

Stephen Elkins

"I am the Way,___ the Truth and the Life.___ No one comes_ to the Fa-

- ther ex-cept_through___ me. "I am the Way, the Truth and the Life.___

No one comes_ to the Fa - ther ex- cept_ through me."___ Je-sus said

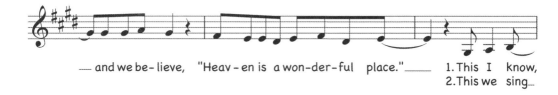

___ and we be-lieve, "Heav-en is a won-der-ful place."___ 1. This I know,
2. This we sing___

___ this I know.___ Heav-en is a won-der-ful place
___ this we sing.___ Heav-en is a won-der-ful place

D.C. al Coda

—— where be - liev - ers in Je - sus go. King.
—— – where Je - sus is Lord___ and

"I am the Way, the Truth and the Life."___

"I am the Way,___ the Truth and the Life."___

MY AFFIRMATION:
I will stay close to Jesus!

73

37 Love Your Neighbor

Stephen Elkins

with a triplet feel

Love,   love,   la, la, la la___ la, love___ your neigh-bor as your-

self.   Love,   love,   la, la, la, la,___ la, love___ your neigh-bor as your

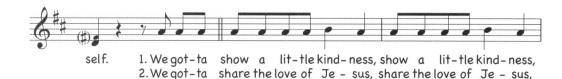

self.   1. We got-ta show a lit-tle kind-ness, show a lit-tle kind-ness,
         2. We got-ta share the love of Je - sus, share the love of Je - sus,

Show the world we real-ly   care.___   Let the love of Je-sus find us,
Share it with eve - ry -one.___   And may eve-ry-one who sees us,

love of Je-sus find us, Sing of His love___   — eve-ry- where.___
eve-ry-one who sees us, Open their hearts___   and love the Son.___

self.   Love your neigh-bor   as   your -

self.   Love your neigh-bor as   your - self.

The Reason We Sing:

Jesus said the most important commandment in the Bible
is to love God. Then He added, "The second is like it.
Love your neighbor as yourself." When asked, "Who is
my neighbor?" Jesus answered with the parable of
the good Samaritan found in Luke 10. We are to
show the love of Jesus to everyone we meet.

MY AFFIRMATION:
I will show love
to others!

38 I Will Make You Fishers of Men

Stephen Elkins

opt. lower harm.

"Come, fol-low me,____ and I will make you fish

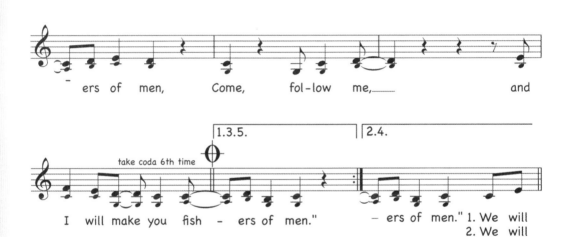

- ers of men, Come, fol-low me,____ and

1.3.5.

take coda 6th time

I will make you fish - ers of men."

2.4.

— ers of men." 1. We will
2. We will

catch them with_ our kind - ness. We will catch them with_ the love_
catch them with_ the gos - pel. We will catch them with_ the grace

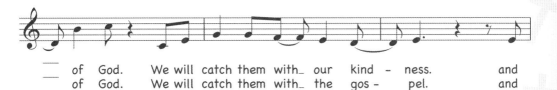

of God. We will catch them with_ our kind - ness. and
of God. We will catch them with_ the gos - pel. and

|1.   D.C. |2.   D.C. al Coda

bring them to the Lord be - cause   He   said: said:
bring them to the Lord be - cause   He

— ers of men."   and   I   will make you   fish - ers of men."

The Reason We Sing:

Jesus said that we should follow Him. To do that, we must stop following the people of this world. We no longer seek fortune and fame, but rather we seek first the kingdom of God. And by following Him, we will show others how to live like Jesus. That's being a true "fisherman" for the Lord!

39 Deep and Wide

Traditional

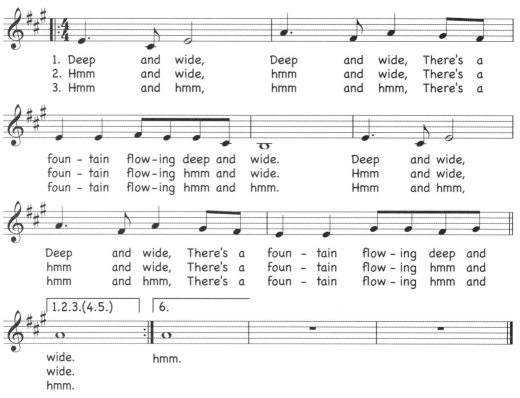

1. Deep and wide, Deep and wide, There's a
2. Hmm and wide, hmm and wide, There's a
3. Hmm and hmm, hmm and hmm, There's a

foun - tain flow-ing deep and wide. Deep and wide,
foun - tain flow-ing hmm and wide. Hmm and wide,
foun - tain flow-ing hmm and hmm. Hmm and hmm,

Deep and wide, There's a foun - tain flow - ing deep and
hmm and wide, There's a foun - tain flow - ing hmm and
hmm and hmm, There's a foun - tain flow - ing hmm and

1.2.3.(4.5.) | **6.**

wide. hmm.
wide.
hmm.

Vs. 4
Hmm and hmm, hmm and hmm
There's a hmm hmm flowing hmm and hmm.
Hmm and hmm, hmm and hmm,
There's a hmm hmm flowing hmm and hmm.

Vs. 5
Hmm and hmm, hmm and hmm
There's a hmm hmm hmm hmm hmm and hmm.
Hmm and hmm, hmm and hmm,
Theres a hmm hmm hmm hmm hmm and hmm.

Vs. 6
Hmm hmm hmm, hmm hmm hmm,
Hmm hmm hmm hmm hmm hmm hmm hmm hmm.
Hmm hmm hmm, hmm hmm hmm,
Hmm hmm hmm hmm hmm hmm hmm hmm hmm.

The Reason We Sing:

How deep and wide is the love of God? In his letter to the Ephesian church, Paul prays that the believers would come to understand, "what is the length and width, height and depth of God's love, and to know the love of Christ that surpasses knowledge." We may not be able to measure it, but we can be sure God loves us more than anything else!

MY AFFIRMATION:

I know God's love is deep and wide!

40 Isn't He Wonderful

Traditional

Is - n't He won-der-ful, won-der - ful, won-der- ful; Is - n't

Je - sus my Lord won - der - ful? Eyes have

seen, ears have heard, it's re - cor - ded in God's word; Is - n't

Je - sus my Lord won - der - ful?

Is - n't ful?

The Reason We Sing:

Jesus promised us that if we take care of the things that are important to God, God will take care of the things that are important to us! What is important to God? He wants us to love Him and come to Him in prayer; He wants us to love one another; He wants us to tell others about His love.

MY AFFIRMATION:

I will do the things that are important to God!

41 Jesus Loves the Little Children

Herbert Woolston
George Root

with a triplet feel

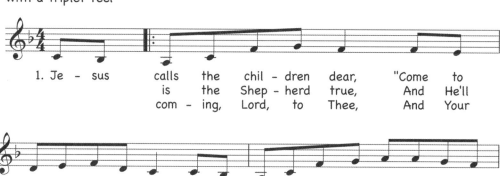

1. Je - sus calls the chil - dren dear, "Come to
   is the Shep - herd true, And He'll
   com - ing, Lord, to Thee, And Your

me and nev - er fear, For I love the lit - tle chil - dren of the
al - ways stand by you, For He loves the lit - tle chil - dren of the
sol - dier I will be, For You love the lit - tle chil - dren of the

world; I will take you by the hand, Lead you
world; He's a Sav - ior great and strong, And He'll
world; And Your cross I'll al - ways bear, And for

to the bet - ter land, For I love the lit - tle chil-dren of the
shield you from the wrong, For He loves the lit - tle chil-dren of the
You I'll do and dare, For You love the lit - tle chil-dren of the

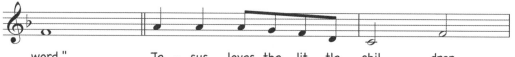

word." Je - sus loves the lit - tle chil - dren,
world. (alt. refrain) Je - sus died for all the chil - dren,
world.

All the chil-dren of the world. Red and yel-low, black and white, All are
All the chil-dren of the world. Red and yel-low, black and white, All are

pre-cious in His sight, Je - sus loves the lit - tle chil-dren of the
pre-cious in His sight, Je - sus died for all the chil-dren of the

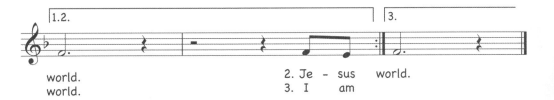

1.2.

world.
world.

2. Je - sus world.
3. I am

3.

The Reason We Sing:

Once when Jesus was teaching, his disciples wouldn't let the children go to Him. They thought Jesus was too busy for children. But Jesus said, "Leave the children alone, and don't try to keep them from coming to me, because the kingdom of heaven is made up of people like this."

MY AFFIRMATION:

I know I'm important to Jesus!

42 I've Got the Joy, Joy, Joy, Joy

Traditional

1. I've got the joy,___ joy,___ joy,___ joy,___
2. I've got the love of Je - sus, love of Je - sus,

down in my heart, where? Down in my heart, where?
down in my heart, where? Down in my heart, where?

Down in my heart, I've got the joy,___ joy,___ joy,___ joy,___
Down in my heart, I've got the love of Je - sus, love of Je - sus,

down in my heart, where? Down in my heart to
down in my heart, where? Down in my heart to

stay.___ And I'm so hap - py,___ so ver - y hap - py. I've
stay.___

got the love of Je-sus in my   heart._And I'm so hap py,_ so ver-y hap-py.   I've

1.2.3.   **4.**

got the love of Je-sus in my   heart.   2. I've got the   heart.
3. I've got the
4. And   if the

Vs. 3
I've got the peace that passes understanding
way down in the depths of my heart, where?
Way down in the depths of my heart, where?
Way down in the depths of my heart.
I've got the peace that passes understanding
way down in the depths of my heart, where?
Way down in the depths of my heart to stay.

Vs. 4
And if the Devil doesn't like it he can
sit on a tack, ouch!
Sit on a tack, ouch!
Sit on a tack,
And if the Devil doesn't like it he can
sit on a tack, ouch!
Sit on a tack to stay!

The Reason We Sing:

Every time I receive a gift, I get so excited! I love
getting presents on my birthday, or at Christmas. It
just fills my heart with joy! Did you know God has
given you a very special gift? It says so in the Bible,
"The gift of God is eternal life!" What's that? You
are going to live forever with Jesus in heaven.

MY AFFIRMATION:

I have joy because of God's gift of eternal life!

43 Father Abraham

Traditional

with a triplet feel

Fa-ther A-bra-ham had ma-ny sons, ma-ny sons had Fa-ther

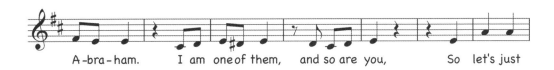

A-bra-ham. I am one of them, and so are you, So let's just

praise the Lord. Right arm! Fa-ther Lord. Right arm, left arm! Fa-ther

Lord. Right arm, left arm, right leg! Fa-ther

Lord. Right arm, left arm, right leg, left leg! Fa-ther

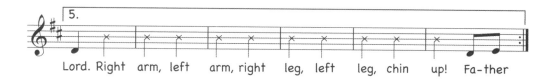

5. Lord. Right arm, left arm, right leg, left leg, chin up! Fa-ther

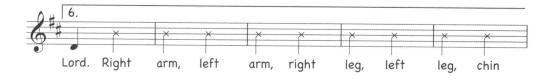

6. Lord. Right arm, left arm, right leg, left leg, chin

up, turn a -round! Fa-ther **7.** Lord. Right arm, left arm, right

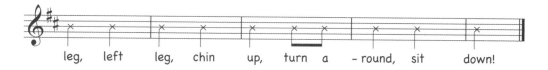

leg, left leg, chin up, turn a - round, sit down!

The Reason We Sing:

Abraham believed God. When God promised him a son, Abraham believed even though he was very old. And God kept his promise! When Abraham was 100 years old, he had a baby boy. Abraham and Sarah named their son Isaac, which in Hebrew means "laughter"!

44 I Love Him Better Every D-A-Y

Stephen Elkins

I love Him bet-ter eve-ry   D -A - Y;   I love Him bet-ter eve-ry

D - A - Y!   He is my Lord, the W -   -   A - Y;

I love Him bet-ter eve-ry   D - A - Y!   I   Love

J -E -S -U -S;   I   know   J -E -S -U -S;

I   need   J -E -S -U -S;   I love Him bet-ter eve-ry

D - A - Y!   D - A - Y!   J - E - S -U -S, I love

J - E - S -U -S! I know   J - E - S -U -S, I need

J - E - S - U - S!   I love Him bet-ter eve-ry

D - A - Y;   I love Him bet-ter eve-ry   D - A - Y.

He is my Lord, the W - - A - Y;

I love Him bet - ter eve - ry   D - A - Y!

45 I Am a C-H-R-I-S-T-I-A-N

Anonymous

1.3. I am a C, I am a C H, I am a
L, I love the L O, I love the

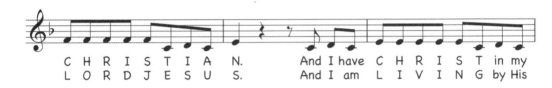

C H R I S T I A N. And I have C H R I S T in my
L O R D J E S U S. And I am L I V I N G by His

H___E A R T and I will L I V E E T E R
W - - O R D and I will N E V E R R E G

1.2.3.
N A L L Y. 2.4. I love the R E T I T.
R E T I T. 3. I am a

4.

Optional verses:
Add "op" to consonants: I am a Cop, I am a Cop Hop, I am a Cop Hop Rop I Sop
Top I A Nop, etc...

The Reason We Sing:

The Bible says that the disciples of Jesus were first called Christians at the church in Antioch. Paul and Barnabas explained to the believers there what it meant to be a Christian. A Christian believes that they are not saved by doing good works but rather by the good work Christ did on the cross. It is by grace we are saved, not by works. That's what it means to be a Christian.

MY AFFIRMATION:

I am a Christian because I trust in Jesus Christ!

46 We Are Climbing Jacob's Ladder

Traditional

We are climb-ing Ja-cob's lad-der,

We are climb-ing Ja-cob's lad-der,

We are climb-ing Ja-cob's lad-der, Sol-diers

of the cross._____ cross._____

Vs. 2 Every rung goes higher, higher . . .
Vs. 3 Seeker, do you love my Jesus? . . .
Vs. 4 If you know Him, why not serve Hiim? . . .
Vs. 5 Seeking, knowing, loving, serving . . .

The Reason We Sing:

Jacob was far from his home and family. He was traveling to a different country. One night as he slept, God sent Jacob a very strange dream. In the dream were steps reaching all the way to heaven. God promised Jacob that He would watch over him wherever he went.

MY AFFIRMATION:

I know God watches over me!

47 My God Is So Big

Traditional

My God is so big, so strong and so might-y, there's noth-ing my

God can-not do. (clap clap) My God is so great, so

strong and so might-y, there's noth-ing my God can-not do. (clap

clap). The moun-tains are His, the riv-ers are His, The

stars are His hand-i-work, too. My God is so great, so

strong and so might-y, there's noth-ing my God can-not do for

1.
you!

2.
My you!

The Reason We Sing:

Is there anything too hard for God to do? Can He heal the sick? No problem! Raise the dead? No problem! Walk on water? No problem! Help me with my test tomorrow? Oops! Is that problem too small for our really big God? Absolutely not! Our God will help us with any problem, big or small!

MY AFFIRMATION:

No problem is too big or small for my God!

48 This Little Light of Mine

Traditional

This lit-tle light of mine, I'm gon-na let it shine.

This lit-tle light of mine, I'm gon-na let it shine.

This lit-tle light of mine, I'm gon-na let it shine, Let it

shine, Let it shine, Let it shine._____

1. Hide it un-der a bush-el? No! I'm gon-na let it shine.
2. Don't let Sa- tan blow it out!
3. Shine it o-ver the whole wide world.
4. Let it shine 'til Je-sus comes.

Hide it un-der a bush-el? No! I'm gon-na let it shine.
Don't let Sa- tan blow it out!
Shine it o-ver the whole wide world.
Let it shine__ 'til Je - sus comes.

Hide it un-der a bush-el? No! I'm gon-na let it shine, Let it
Don't let Sa- tan blow it out!
Shine it o-ver the whole wide world.
Let it shine__ 'til Je - sus comes.

4th time D.C. al Coda
1.2.3.4.

shine, Let it shine, Let is shine._____   shine._____

The Reason We Sing:

Psalm 119 says that God's Word is like a lamp that shines light on our path. It shows us the way. It shows us dangers that need to be avoided. When we memorize a Bible verse, it becomes a little light hidden in our heart. When we remember the words, and live by them each day, we become "lights" to the world. Showing kindness, and patience, and love to others causes us to shine!

49 Do Lord

1. I've got a home in glo - ry land that out-shines the sun.
2. I took_ Je - sus as my Sav - ior, you take Him, too.

I've got a home in glo - ry land that out-shines the sun.
I took_ Je - sus as my Sav - ior, you take Him, too.

I've got a home in glo - ry land that out-shines the sun._____
I took Je - sus as my Sav - ior, you take Him, too._____

Way be - yond_____ the blue.
Way be - yond_____ the blue.

Do Lord, O, Do Lord, O, do re-mem - ber me.

Do Lord, O, Do Lord, O, do re-mem - ber me.

Do Lord, O, Do Lord, O, do re-mem - ber me.____

opt. lower harm.

1.   2.

Way be - yond____ the blue.   blue.

The Reason We Sing:

I wonder how God will remember everybody's name when we get to heaven. Do you think he might forget about you? The Bible says in Psalm 105 that God remembers His promises. And in Psalm 145 it says that God is faithful to keep all of His promises. If you have believed in Jesus, God has promised you heaven. He will not forget!

MY AFFIRMATION:
I know God remembers me!

50 Children, Obey Your Parents

Stephen Elkins

Chil-dren, o-bey your par-ents in the Lord, for this is right. Chil-dren, o-bey your par-ents in the Lord, for this is right.

take coda third time

Hon-or your fath-er and moth-er, Which is the first com-mand-ment with a prom-ise That it may go well with you And that you

1.2. 2nd time D.C. al Coda

may en-joy long life___ on the earth right.

The Reason We Sing:

It's hard to believe sometimes, but rules were made to keep us safe. Your mom and dad don't want to spoil your fun by telling you, "Don't play in the street." They just don't want you to get hit by a car. And just like your parents have rules, God has rules that everyone should obey. These rules are in the Bible. They're called the Ten Commandments. Like a good father, God knows what's best for us!

MY AFFIRMATION:

I will obey my parents because they know what's best!

51 The Lord Is My Shepherd

Stephen Elkins

The Lord is, the Lord is__ my Shep- herd,_ The Lord is, the

Lord is__ my Shep-herd; I shall not be in want, na na na__ na na na. The

Lord is, the Lord is__ my Shep- herd, The Lord is, the

Lord is__ my Shep-herd; I shall not be in want, na na na__ na na na. The

take Coda
3rd time

Lord is__ my Shep-herd; I shall not be in want.

1. He leads me be-side still__ wa - ters; He re-stores my
2. He makes me lie down in green pas - tures; He re-stores my

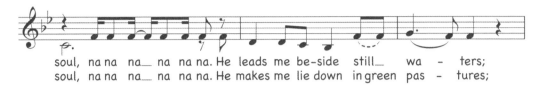

soul, na na na__ na na na. He leads me be-side still__ wa - ters;
soul, na na na__ na na na. He makes me lie down in green pas - tures;

He re - stores my soul. The soul. The
He re - stores my

The Reason We Sing:

Most of us live in cities and towns and don't know much about sheep. But a good shepherd will take care of his sheep. He makes sure the sheep have good food to eat and water to drink. A good shepherd protects his flock and keeps them safe. That's why the Bible calls the Lord our shepherd. He loves us, provides for our needs, guides us, and protects us just like a shepherd who cares for his sheep!

52 In the Beginning

Stephen Elkins

Gen - e - sis,   Gen - e - sis!   Verse one, one, verse one, one!

take Coda
4th time

In the be-gin-ning God cre-a-ted   the heav- ens and the earth.   1. Day
2. Day
3. Day

(yelling on vs. 2)

one, He made the light, _   _   dark-ness did   a - bound.   He
three, guess what He made? _   _   Sail - ors shout "Hoo- ray!"   The
five, He made the spar-rows   and   eve - ry bird that flies.   And

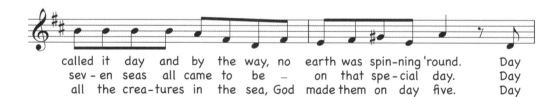

called it   day   and by   the way, no earth was spin-ning 'round.   Day
sev - en seas all came to   be _   on that spe-cial   day.   Day
all the crea-tures in   the sea, God made them on day   five.   Day

two, He made the wa - ters,   it's e nough to laugh.
four, He made the stars shine,   the sun, and moon above.   In
six, He made the an - i - mals, the big and small, you see.   And

1.

I'm re - mind- ed eve - ry time I have to take a bath!

2.

heav-en's light on star - ry nights I see our Fa - ther's love.

3.   D.C. al Coda

on that day hip, hip, hoo- ray!_   God made Ad-am and Eve.

the heav - ens and the earth.   the heav - ens and the earth.

53 Glorify the Lord with Me

Stephen Elkins

Glor - i - fy, glo - ri - fy___ the Lord with me.

Glo - ri - fy, glo -ri- fy___ the Lord with me. Let us___ ex-alt His

name to - geth - er, Let us___ ex-alt His name for-ev - er. Oh,___

take coda 3rd time

Glo - ri - fy, glo -ri fy___ the Lord with me. glo -ri fy___ the Lord, our

Lord. In eve - ry- thing___ you say, glo - ri -

fy the Lord._ Eve-ry night_ and day glo - ri - fy the Lord._ In

all that_ you do, let His glo - ry_ shine through. Oh,

1.

2. D.C. al Coda

glo-ri- fy_ the Lord with me. me. Lord.

The Reason We Sing:

To "glorify the Lord" is to make His name known among the people. It's like giving God the credit for everything wonderful in your life. When you see a beautiful sunrise, glorify the Lord; give Him the credit for making it. When you are blessed with health and happiness, glorify the Lord. Come on and glorify the Lord with me!

MY AFFIRMATION:

I will glorify the name of the Lord!

54 I Know the Plans I Have for You

Stephen Elkins

opt. lower harm.

"For   I know   the plans I have for you,_ my lit-tle chil-dren,

For   I know   your plans,"de- clares the Lord.   Plans to pros - per you and

not to harm_ you, no! Plans to give_you hope and a fu-ture that_will grow!_

Then   you will call_ up - on me, come and pray_ to me, me!

And   I will lis - ten to you, that's how it_ should be!

"For I know the plans I have for you, my lit-tle chil-dren, For I know your plans," de-clares the Lord. Plans to pros-per you and not to harm you, no! Plans to give you hope and a fu-ture that will grow! "For I know the plans I have for you, my lit-tle chil-dren, For I know your plans," de-clares the Lord. "Your plans," de-clares the Lord; "Your plans," de-clares the Lord.

MY AFFIRMATION:

I know the Lord has a plan for my life!

55 Hidden in My Heart

Stephen Elkins

I have hid-den Your word in my heart

That I might not sin a-gainst You, Lord,

Yes, I have hid-den Your word, Lord, Deep in my

heart So that I can re - mem - ber

all the words of grace; So that I

1.

can re - mem - ber and al - ways

seek   Your   face._____

ber   All   the   words   of   grace.   all   the

words   of   grace,   All   the   words   of   grace.

The Reason We Sing:

When Jesus was tempted in the wilderness, He answered Satan by quoting Bible verses. Psalm 119 says we "hide the word in our hearts." This means we are able to remember what the Bible says. The same verse goes on to say, "so that I won't sin against You." We remember what the Bible says, so we know the right thing to do … just like Jesus!

MY AFFIRMATION:

I will remember what God's word says!

56 The Roman's Road

Stephen Elkins

For all have sinned and fall short of the glo-ry of God. For

all have sinned and fall short of the glo-ry of God. For the

wag-es of sin is death, but the gift of God is e-ter-nal life__ through

take Coda
3rd time

Je-sus Christ.__ But

God dem-on-strates__ His own love for us__ in

this while we were still sin-ners Christ died for us.__ But

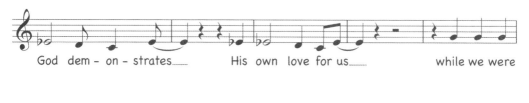

God dem - on - strates___ His own love for us___ while we were

still sin - ners Christ died for us For

For

The Reason We Sing:

Paul wrote in Romans, "The wages of sin are death." Wages are payment for something we do. The payment for work is money; the payment for sin is death. Paul goes on to say, "but the gift of God is eternal life." A gift is not something we earn, it is given. Paul was teaching us that we don't earn eternal life. We receive it by faith as a gift from God.

MY AFFIRMATION:

I will receive God's gift of eternal life!

57 For God So Loved the World

Stephen Elkins

For God so loved the world, God so loved the world; God so loved the world, He gave His on - ly Son. That who - so - ev - er be - liev - eth, in Him, in Him; Should not per - ish but have e - ter - nal life, a - men! For Son.

The Reason We Sing:

Who is God? What is he like? These questions can be answered with a single word: Love! God is love. His love doesn't depend on what we do. He always loves the sinner, but he doesn't love sin. In fact, His heart is broken by it. But John 3:16 says, "For God so loved the world that he gave his only Son." Jesus would die on a cross to give us eternal life. Now that's real love!

MY AFFIRMATION:

I know God loves me!

58 When I Am Afraid

Stephen Elkins

When   I am a - fraid,____ I will trust in You,   I will trust in You,

— my Fa - ther____ When   I am a - fraid,___ I will trust in You,

take coda 3rd time

I will trust in You,__ O Lord__ my__ God.____

1. No sit - u - a - tion,   no ag-gra-va - tion Is be - yond my Lord,
2. No cir-cum - stan - ces, when fear ad-van - ces Call up - on___ the Lord,

— my Lord.   In my con-fu - sion, the real so - lu - tion is
— my Lord.   He's like a fa - ther, __ like no oth - er keep

trust-ing in___ His Ho - ly Word.___
trust-ing in___ His Ho - ly Word.___

— O Lord my___ God,

O Lord my___ God,

The Reason We Sing:

Have you ever been afraid? We all have! Everyone is afraid every now and then. Maybe you heard a strange noise in your room. Or perhaps you imagined you saw something moving in the dark. Nothing calms a fearful heart like a friend with a confident voice saying, "It's okay. I'm here with you." God is that confident friend. He answers us when we are afraid. So call on the Lord in your time of trouble.

59 Come to Me

Stephen Elkins

half time triplet feel

"Come to me,— O come— to me,— all you who are wear - y

Come to me,— O come— to me,— all you who are bur - dened and

I will give— you rest,— I will give— you rest,— I will

take coda 3rd time

give you rest."

1. When the bur-den seems un - bear
2. He's the Lord now and— for - ev -

- a-ble, what can you do?— You need a friend to
- er — He'll nev-er change— — He's the one who

come and help you through.___   I have found a friend_ in Je
knows your eve - ry   need.___   I have found a friend_ in Je

\- sus,   so   faith - ful   and   true.___   — And the
\- sus,   He   knows right   a - way.___   And if   you

| 1. | 2.D.C. al Coda |

prom-ise that_ He made___ I   sing to   you:
lis - ten close,_ I   know___ you'll hear Him say:

"I   will   give   you rest.

I   will   give   you rest."

MY AFFIRMATION:

God will give me rest!

60 The Fruit of the Spirit

Stephen Elkins

1. The fruit of the Spir - it is love, joy and peace.

The   A - gainst such things_ there is   no   law,

no   law,   none at all.   A - gainst such things_ there is   no   law,

glo - ry to our God.   2. The

fruit of the Spir - it is   pa - tience, kind - ness and good - ness.

The   A - gainst such things_ there is   no   law,

no law, none at all. A - gainst such things＿there is no law,

glo - ry to our God.   3. The

fruit of the Spir- it is faith-ful-ness, gen-tle-ness and self con- trol.＿

1.   2.   D.S. al Coda

The   A -   God.

The fruit of the Spir - it is

rit.

love, joy and peace.

61 God Works for the Good

Stephen Elkins

And we know— that in all things God works for the good—— of

those who love Him. And we know— that in all things God

works for the good—— of those who love—— Him.

1. God has giv-en a prom-ise and I know it is true.—
2. God has giv-en a prom-ise I will trust in the Lord.—

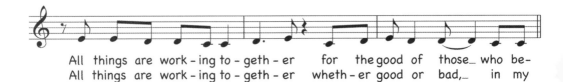

All things are work-ing to-geth-er for the good of those— who be-
All things are work-ing to-geth-er wheth-er good or bad,— in my

lieve, do you?___   Yes, I do!
heart I'm sure.___   Yes, I'm sure!

And we know___ that in all things   And we know___ that in

all things   And we know___ that in all things

The Reason We Sing:

When you become a Christian you are given an amazing promise. The promise is this: no matter what happens to you, whether good or bad, God is using the events of your life to make you a better person. But you have a promise. God is working for your good, no matter what. Just believe in His promise!

MY AFFIRMATION:
God is always there to help me!

62 The Lord Is My Rock

Stephen Elkins

1. I love You, O Lord, my strength, my re-deem-er. I Love You, O Lord, my
   praise You, O Lord, my strength, my re-deem er. I praise You, O Lord, my

for-tress, my all.___ I love You, O Lord, my strength, my re-deem-er, so
for-tress, my all.___ I praise You, O Lord, my strength, my re-deem-er, so

thank-ful You hear_ me call. O the Lord is my rock, I will roll___ to Him.___
thank-ful You hear_ me call.

Time and a-gain_ He has helped me through. O, the Lord is my rock, On your life_

opt. upper harm.

1.

___ de-pend._ He's the rock, you can roll___ to___ Him.

2.

2. I Him. When trouble comes,_ you can

roll to Him;__ your bus-ted bub-ble comes,__ roll to Him. When

bad news breaks you can roll to Him; He is your clos-est friend!__ O the

Him. O the Lord is my rock, I will roll__ to Him.

Time and a - gain__ He has helped me through. O, the Lord is my rock, On your life

__ de - pend.__ He's the rock, you can roll__ to__ Him. He's the

rock, you can roll__ to__ Him. He's the rock, you can roll__ to__ Him.

MY AFFIRMATION: The Lord is my rock!

63 J-O-Y

Stephen Elkins

Joy,   joy,   J -O -Y,___ Oh, I___ will sing of Joy,   joy,

J -O -Y,___ Oh, I___ will sing. Make mu - sic to the Lord,___

I will sac-ri-fice with Joy,   joy,   J -O -Y,___ Oh I___ just shout with

1.   2.3.

joy.   joy.   Deep down___ in-side I got a lit-tle

love I___ can't hide when - ev - er___ I sing of the

(opt. group 2)

Lord doo doot doot_ doot doo doo doot Down in___ my heart I got a lit-tle

love rea-dy___ to start. When ev - er___ I sing of___ the

Lord. doo doot doot_ doot doo doo doot

Lord. doo doot doot_ doot doo doo doot

Joy, joy, J -O -Y,___ Oh, I___ will sing of Joy, joy,

J - O -Y,___ Oh, I___ will sing. Make mu - sic to the Lord,

I will sac-ri-fice with Joy, joy, J -O -Y,___ Oh I___ just shout with

Joy, joy, J -O - Y,___ Oh I___ just shout with

Joy, joy, J -O -Y,___ Oh I___ just shout with Joy,

64 Let Everything that Has Breath

Stephen Elkins

1. Let eve-ry - thing,— eve-ry-thing that has breath,

let eve-ry- thing,— eve-ry-thing that has breath

praise the Lord, praise the Lord I say, can you hear me to- day?—

take coda 2nd time

Come on, eve-ry girl and boy, make a might-y noise and praise the

Lord. 2. Let eve-ry-

thing,— eve-ry-thing that has breath, let eve-ry

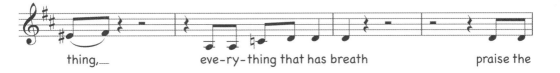

thing,—   eve-ry-thing that has breath   praise the

Lord, praise the Lord with   me,   till   all the world can   see.—

He's a great and might-y God so where-e'er your feet may trod, praise the

Lord.   Let eve-ry-   Lord.

The Reason We Sing:

Take a deep breath. Okay, that's good! Now breathe out. Excellent! You qualify as a person who has breath according to the Psalmist. David writes, "Let everything (that includes you) who has breath, 'Praise the Lord!'" We praise the Lord and thank Him for the breath that fills our lungs. For He has made all things possible in His awesome creation. So let's praise the Lord!

65 What Is Impossible with Men

Stephen Elkins

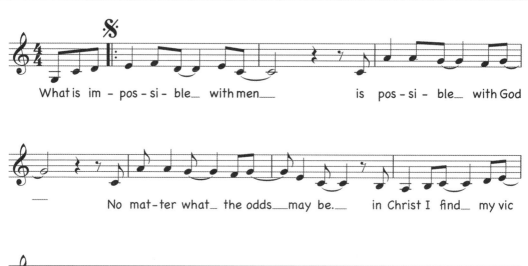

What is im - pos - si - ble__ with men__ is pos - si - ble__ with God

__ No mat-ter what__ the odds__ may be.__ in Christ I find__ my vic

- to - ry. What is im - pos - si - ble__ with men__ is

pos - si - ble__ with God__ my friend.__ Through it all, come

thick or thin__ I'll be - lieve it's pos - si - ble__ with Him.

1. Too hard?   Noth-ing can be.___   Too hard?
2. Too big?   Is an-y-thing?___   Too big?   For

If you be - lieve.___   God will   an - swer me
Je-sus our king.___   Noth- ing   He can't do

1.   **D.S.**

If I pray and I be-lieve.___   What is im -
Just be-lieve, God's word is true.___

2.   **D.S. al Coda**

What is im -

The Reason We Sing:

In God's kingdom, nothing is impossible. As a matter of fact, *all* things are possible with Him. There is *nothing* God can't do! He heals the sick and raises the dead. He can even part a sea if necessary to save His children. Some say, "God doesn't do miracles any more." To them the Bible says, "Without faith it is *impossible* to please God." All things are possible if we have faith in God!

131

66 I Will Sing of the Mercies

Psalm 89:1
James Fillmore

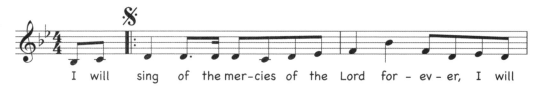

I will sing of the mer-cies of the Lord for - ev - er, I will

sing, I will sing, I will sing of the mer-cies of the

take Coda
3rd time

Lord for - ev - er, I will sing of the mer-cies of the Lord. With my

mouth___ will I make known Thy faith-ful-ness, Thy faith-ful-ness, With my

mouth_____ will I make known Thy faith-ful-ness to all gen-er-

1.   2.   D.S. al Coda

a - tions. I will a - tions. I will Lord.

The Reason We Sing:

God shows mercy by sparing some the punishment they truly deserve. God shows mercy because He loves us. So when we sing of God's mercy, we sing of His love! Although we have disobeyed Him in so many ways, He does not give us the punishment we deserve. He shows us mercy and love. The Bible says, "According to His great mercy, He saved us."

MY AFFIRMATION:

I will sing of God's mercy!

67 The Lord's Prayer

Stephen Elkins

Our Fa-ther, which art in heav-en, hal-low-ed be Thy name.

name. Thy king-dom come, Thy will be done on earth as it is in

heav-en. Thy king-dom come, Thy will be done on earth as it is in

heav-en. Give us this day our dai - ly

bread and give us this day our dai - ly bread.

Our Fa-ther, which art in heav-en, hal-low-ed be Thy name.

Our Fa-ther, which art in heav-en, hal-low-ed be Thy name.

name. And lead us not in - to temp-ta- tion, de-liv-er us from e- vil. For

Thine is the po-wer and the glo-ry for ev-er and ev - er.

Our Fa-ther, which art in heav-en, hal-low-ed be Thy

name. name. hal-low-ed be Thy name.

MY AFFIRMATION:

I know that "hallowed" means
to respect or honor greatly!

68 The Star-Spangled Banner

Francis Scott Key
John Stafford Smith

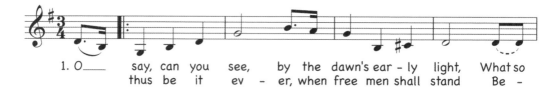

1. O___ say, can you see, by the dawn's ear - ly light, What so
   thus be it ev - er, when free men shall stand Be -

proud - ly we hailed at the twi-light's last gleam-ing, Whose broad
tween their loved homes and the war's des - o - la - tion! Blest with

stripes and bright stars, through the per - il - ous fight, O'er the
vic - t'ry and peace, may the heav'n res - cued land Praise the

ram - parts we watched, were so gal - lant - ly stream-ing? And the
Pow'r that hath made and pre - served us a na - tion! Then_

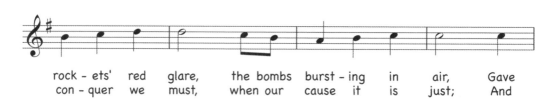

rock - ets' red glare, the bombs burst - ing in air, Gave
con - quer we must, when our cause it is just; And

proof through the night that our flag was still there. O___
this be our mot - to: "In God is our trust!" And the

say, does that_ star-span-gled ban - ner_ yet_ wave_ O'er the
star - span- gled_ ban - ner in tri - umph shall_ wave_ O'er the

1.

land_____ of the free and the home of the brave?
land_____ of the free and the home of the

2.

2. O_____ brave!

69 God Bless America

Irving Berlin

While the storm clouds gath-er   far a-cross the sea,

Let us swear al - le-giance   to a land that's free.

Let us all be grate-ful   for a land so fair,

As we raise our voic-es   in a sol-emn prayer._____

opt. upper harm.

God bless A - mer-i-ca,   Land that I love,   Stand be-

side her   and   guide her   Through the night with a light from a -

bove.   From the moun - tains,   to   the prai - ries,   To the

2nd time opt. upper harm.

o - ceans white with foam.   God   bless A - mer-i-ca,   My

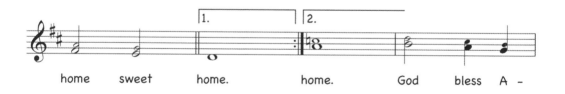

1.   2.

home   sweet   home.   home.   God   bless A -

mer - i - ca,   my   home   sweet   home.

70 America the Beautiful

Katharine Bates
Samuel Ward

1. O beau - ti - ful for spa - cious skies, For
   beau - ti - ful for pil - grim feet, Whose
   beau - ti - ful for he - roes proved In
   beau - ti - ful for pa - triot dream That

am - ber waves of grain, For pur - ple moun - tain
stern im - pas - sioned stress A thor - ough - fare for
lib - er - at - ing strife, Who more than self their
sees be - yond the years Thine al - a - bas - ter

maj - es - ties A - bove the fruit - ed
free - dom beat A - cross the wil - der -
coun - try loved, And mer - cy more than
cit - ies gleam, Un - dimmed by hu - man

opt. lower harm.

plain! A - mer - i - ca! A - mer - i - ca! God
ness! A - mer - i - ca! A - mer - i - ca! God
life! A - mer - i - ca! A - mer - i - ca! May
tears! A - mer - i - ca! A - mer - i - ca! God

shed	His	grace	on		thee,	And	crown	thy good	with
mend	thine	eve -	ry		flaw,	Con -	firm	thy soul	in
God	thy	gold	re -		fine,	Till	all	suc-cess	be
shed	His	grace	on		thee,	And	crown	thy good	with

broth	–	er -	hood	From	sea	to	shin	–	ing
self	–	con -	trol,	Thy	lib	–	er	–	ty	in
no	–	ble -	ness,	And	eve	–	ry	gain	di	–
broth	–	er -	hood	From	sea	to	shin	–	ing

1.2.3. **4.**

sea!			sea!
law!	2. O	
vine!	3. O	
	4. O	

The Reason We Sing:

America is a beautiful place. We stand in awe as we look across the Grand Canyon. Words cannot describe the power and breathtaking beauty of Niagra Falls. From the snow-capped peaks of the Rockies to the shores of New England, America is beautiful because our God is so beautiful!

71 Christ the Lord Is Risen Today

Charles Wesley
Lyra Davidica, London

1. Christ the Lord is ris'n to - day,____ Al - le -
2. Lives a - gain our glo - rious King,____
3. Love's re - deem - ing work is done,____
4. Soar we now where Christ has led,____

- lu - ia! Sons of men and an - gels say:____
Where, O death, is now thy sting?____
Fought the fight, the bat - tle won,____
Fol - l'wing our ex - alt - ed Head,____

Al - - le - lu - ia! Raise your joys and
Dy - ing once He
Death in vain for -
Made like Him, like

tri - umphs high, Al - - le - lu - ia!
all doth save,
bids Him rise,
Him we rise,

Sing,___ ye___ heav'ns, and earth re - ply___
Where_ thy___ vic - to - ry, O grave?___
Christ_ has___ o - pened Par - a - dise,___
Ours_ the cross, the grave, the skies,___

1.2.3.

Al - - le - lu - ia!

4.

lu - ia! Al - - le - lu - ia!

The Reason We Sing:

The core belief of every Christian is a risen Savior. Jesus Christ was crucified, died, and spent three days in the grave. But on Sunday, when the women came to the tomb to anoint the body, Jesus was not there! "Jesus has risen!" said the angel. Yes, the foundation of Christianity is a risen Savior!

MY AFFIRMATION:
Christ is risen!

72 Do Remember

Stephen Elkins

Do re-mem-ber, do this to re mem-ber; Do re-mem-ber, re

mem-ber what God has done. Do re-mem-ber, do this to re mem-ber;

Do re-mem-ber, re - mem-ber what God has done._____ 1. Take the
2. Take the

1. cup in your hand,_ re-mem-ber Him,_ our Sav-ior who died; O,_____
2. bread in you hand,_ re-mem-ber Him,_ the Bo-dy of Christ; O,_____

1. — Take the cup and do drink,_ and think a- bout_ the
2. — Take the bread and do eat,_ and think a- bout_ His

73 Hosanna

Stephen Elkins

Ho - san - na,   ho - san - na,   ho -

san - na, ho-san-na to the King.   Ho - san - na,   ho -

san - na,   ho - san - na to the King.   O bless - ed,   O

bless - ed,   O   bless - ed, it is He who

comes   1. in the name, glo - ri - ous name, won-der-ful
           2. in the name, beau-ti - ful name, pre - cious
           3. in the name, glo - ri - ous name, won-der-ful

name, mar-vel-ous name; in the might - y name of the
name, ho - ly name; in the might - y name of the
name, mar-vel ous name; in the might - y name of the

1.2.
3.

Lord. Ho - Lord. In the name, glo-ri-ous name, won-der-ful
Lord.

name, mar-vel-ous name; in the might - y name of the Lord.

The Reason We Sing:

As Jesus entered Jerusalem riding on a donkey's back, the people shouted "Hosanna! Hosanna!" which means "Save us, please!" The Jewish leaders knew very well what Hosanna meant and it made them very angry. The people were calling out to Jesus for salvation!

MY AFFIRMATION:
Jesus Saves!

74 Go Tell It on the Mountain

Traditional

with a triplet feel

Go, tell it on the moun - tain, O - ver the hills and

eve - ry - where; Go, tell it on the

moun - tain That Je-sus Christ_ is born.
1. While shep-herds kept their
2. The shep-herds feared and
3. Down in a low - ly

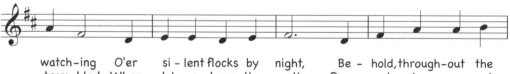

watch-ing O'er si - lent flocks by night, Be - hold, through-out the
trem-bled When, lo! a - bove the earth Rang out he an - gel
man - ger The hum-ble Christ was born And brought us God's sal -

heav-ens   There shone a   ho - ly   light.____   morn.____
cho - rus   That hailed our Sav - ior's   birth.____
va - tion   That bless-ed Christ-mas

born.   Go,   tell it on the moun - tain,

O-ver the hills and   eve - ry - where;   Go,   tell it on the

moun - tain That   Je - sus Christ____ is   born.

MY AFFIRMATION:

I will tell people about Jesus!

75 The First Noel

Traditional
W. Sandy

1. The first Noel, the an-gel did say, Was to
   look-ed up and saw a star Shin-ing
   en - tered in those wise men three, Full
   let us all with one ac - cord Sing

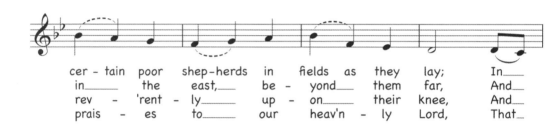

cer - tain poor shep-herds in fields as they lay; In
in the east, be - yond them far, And
rev - 'rent - ly up - on their knee, And
prais - es to our heav'n - ly Lord, That

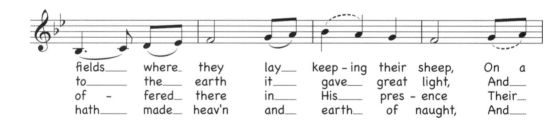

fields where they lay keep - ing their sheep, On a
to the earth it gave great light, And
of - fered there in His pres - ence Their
hath made heav'n and earth of naught, And

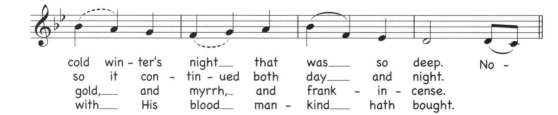

cold win - ter's night that was so deep. No -
so it con - tin - ued both day and night.
gold, and myrrh, and frank - in - cense.
with His blood man - kind hath bought.

el,_____ No - el, No - el, No - el,

opt. lower harm.

Born is the King___ of Is - ra - el.

1.2.3.

4.

2. They___ el.
3. Then___
4. Then___

76 Away in a Manger

Anonymous, Stanza 1-2
John MacFarland, Stanza 3
James Murray

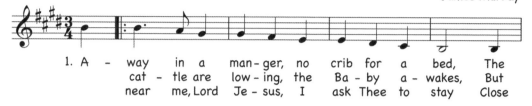

1. A - way in a man - ger, no crib for a bed, The
cat - tle are low - ing, the Ba - by a - wakes, But
near me, Lord Je - sus, I ask Thee to stay Close

lit - tle Lord Je - sus laid down His sweet head; The
lit - tle Lord Je - sus no cry - ing He makes, I
by me for - ev - er, and love me, I pray. Bless

stars in the sky_____ looked down where He
love Thee, Lord Je - sus, look down from the
all the dear chil - dren in Thy ten - der

lay, The lit - tle Lord Je - sus, a - sleep on the
sky, And stay by my cra - dle till morn - ing is
care, And fit us for heav - en, to live with Thee

1.2. **3.**

hay._____ 2. The there._____
nigh._____ 3. Be

The Reason We Sing:

A manger is a strange place for a king to sleep. Kings should sleep in luxury! Who would think of placing a king in a box made of wood used to feed animals? But that's where Jesus spent His first night on earth. God was teaching us humility in the life of His own Son. A manger was the perfect bed for Jesus. He was the humble King.

MY AFFIRMATION:

I will be humble like Jesus!

77 Joy to the World

Isaac Watts
Joseph Handel

1. Joy to the world! the Lord is come; Let
2. Joy to the earth! the Sav - ior reigns; Let
3. He rules the world with truth and grace, And

earth re - ceive her King;_____ Let
men their songs em - ploy;_____ While
makes the na - tions prove_____ The

eve - ry_____ heart_____ pre - pare_____ Him_____
fields_____ and_____ floods,_____ rocks, hills,_____ and_____
glo - ries_____ of_____ His right - eous -

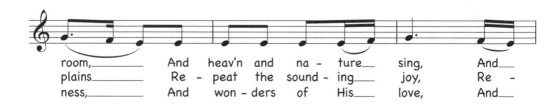

room,_____ And heav'n and na - ture_____ sing, And_____
plains_____ Re - peat the sound - ing_____ joy, Re -
ness,_____ And won - ders of His_____ love, And_____

heav'n and na - ture___ sing, And___ heav'n,___ and
peat the sound - ing___ joy, Re - peat,___ re -
won - ders of His___ love, And___ won - ders,

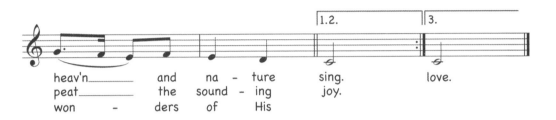

|1.2. |3. |

heav'n___ and na - ture sing. love.
peat___ the sound - ing joy.
won - ders of His

The Reason We Sing:

Jesus fulfilled over 300 prophesies telling of His coming. They said He would be born in Bethlehem; that He would be called a Nazarene; that He would be betrayed by a friend and silent before His accusers. They said He would be crucified.

Every believer can tell you that Jesus brings joy into their lives. It's a joy that comes from knowing that He came to save you and me!

> **MY AFFIRMATION:**
> # I am joyful knowing Jesus is the Messiah!

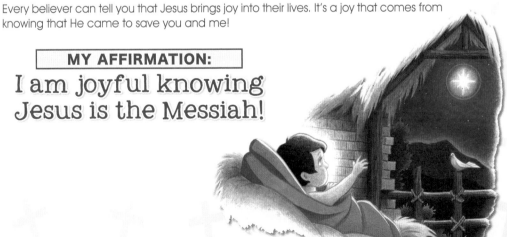

78 O Come, All Ye Faithful

John Frances Wade
translated by Frederick Oakeley

1. O Come, all ye faith - ful, joy - ful and tri -
2. _ Sing, choirs of an - gels, sing in ex - ul -

um - phant, O come, Ye, O come___ ye to
ta - tion, O Sing, all ye cit - i - zens of

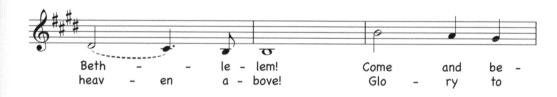

Beth - - le - lem! Come and be -
heav - en a - bove! Glo - ry to

hold Him, born the King of an - gels! O
God, all glo - ry in the high - est!

come, let us a - dore Him, O come, let us a -

dore Him, O come, let us a -

dore Him,___ Christ___ the Lord! Lord!

MY AFFIRMATION:
I will come to the cross and adore Jesus!

79 Children, Go Where I Send Thee

Traditional

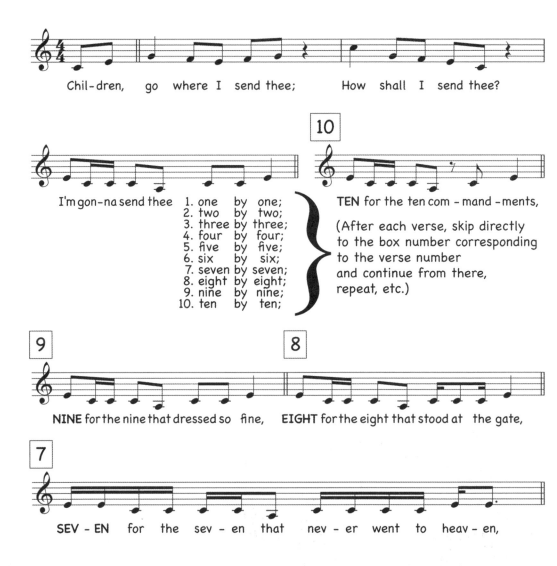

6 SIX for the six that nev-er got fixed,

5 FIVE for the gos-pel preach-ers,

4 FOUR for the four that stood at the door,

3 THREE for the He-brew chil-dren,

2 TWO for Paul and Si - las,

1 ONE for the lit-tle bit-ty ba - by,

Fine
last time D.C.

Born, born, born in Beth - le - hem.

MY AFFIRMATION:
I will go where
God sends me!

159

80 Silent Night

Joseph Mohr
Franz Gruber

1. Si - lent night, ho - ly night, All is calm, all is
2. Si - lent night, ho - ly night, Son of God, love's pure

bright Round yon vir - gin moth - er and Child. Ho - ly
light Ra - diant beams from Thy ho-ly face, With the

In fant so ten-der and mild, Sleep in heav-en-ly peace,
dawn of re - deem - ing grace, Je - sus, Lord, at Thy birth,

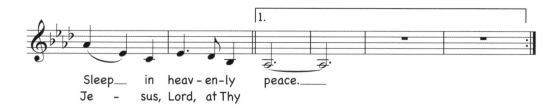

1.

Sleep in heav - en-ly peace.
Je - sus, Lord, at Thy

2.

birth.

The Reason We Sing:

As the shepherds looked upon the face of Jesus, they were silent. A brilliant star shone overhead and angels had heralded His coming. They wondered who this child would become. What would He be like? Where would He live and what would He do? They were silent that night. All they could think of was how wonderful God must be!

MY AFFIRMATION:

In silence we listen for the voice of God.

Title Index

Companion DVD Index

Companion CD Index